To my darling daughter,
Deanna Renee,
my source of inspiration for this book,
and for teenagers everywhere.
Hang in there.
Love,
Angela Shelf Medearis

As Soon As I Find Out Who I Am
You'll Be the First to Know

I promise to send you a letter
or call you on the phone
as soon as I find
myself.
I promise you'll be the first to know.
But right now,
I'm having a hard time
even communicating with me.
I just can't seem to find
a language
or the right words to say,
to talk about my feelings
with you.

I'd Rather

I'd rather walk
over a bed of hot coals
with my bare feet
through a jungle
with snakes dripping off of every tree
and lie on a bed of
carefully sharpened nails
with a 2,000 pound weight on
my chest
than walk through the hall
where all the boys hang out.

Jigsaw

I've been trying so hard to
fit in
that I've lost
parts of myself.

Maintaining an Attitude

I'm having a hard time being cool
posing and
maintaining the right attitude
with
her around.

Friendship

When your two best friends are arguing
and you're right in the middle,
it's best to be best friends
with yourself.

Skin Deep

I wish my skin came
equipped with a zipper
right in the center of my belly button.
Then,
when I see the fear creep into your eyes
and your mind fill up with
all those things your momma told you
and the newspapers told you
and you saw on the TV or heard on the radio
about BLACK people
ZIPPPPPP
I could slip out of my skin.
I'd look just like those pictures in an
anatomy book,
red and blue veins everywhere.
Just another naked human being,
no different than you.

Tennis Shoes

My shoes cost more
than everything else
on my whole body!
Some guys would
cut off my head
just to get
what's on my feet!

The sad thing about it is,
my shoes are probably
not even their size.

The Oldest

After years of cold, unexplained silences
and electric tension
my parents are getting a divorce.
Since I'm
the oldest,
they told me first
so I can help explain it to
my little brothers and sisters.
My only question is,
who's going to explain it
to me?

You Have My Deepest Sympathy As You Go Through Puberty

Your voice shifted between middle G, low F,
and an ear-piercing high C
in just one sentence.
Your body is in a hairy revolt.
You cry and laugh
and laugh and cry
within the space of five minutes.
Your emotions are a roller coaster
of feelings
too hard to express
and too painful to forget.
Your mind is a jumble of weird thoughts
with no explanations,
and no one really understands you.
If they did,
they wouldn't leave you so alone.
But, maybe solitude is a good thing
because your face is a mess anyway.
Insanity?
No, puberty. PUBERTY.
Radical changes in your mind and body
without your consent.
Cheer up,
there are survivors
of this dreaded
dis-ease
they're called . . .
ADULTS.

Modern Dating

I saw her in the hallway.
She was standing by her locker.
I only had a few minutes
to ask her that important question.
"Hi," I said.
"Hi," she said.
"Look," I said. "Uh, um, uh . . ."
"Do you want to go to the dance?" she said.
"Yeah," I said.
"Can you pick me up at eight?"
"Yeah," I said.
"That's great," she said. "I'll see you later."
"Yeah," I said.
Oh, well, I guess I can borrow her history notes
some other time.

Report Card

I'd have an A in algebra
or even a good passing
B
or even a "tried but couldn't quite make it"
C
if good-looking you
weren't seated right next to me.

Dressing Out

I would rather have the mumps than
dress out for gym.
I never wanted to be physically fit anyway.
The worst part about gym
is the stupid gym suits you have to wear.
The tag inside says
"one size fits all,"
all but me I guess.
I look like a baby-blue Polish sausage in that thing.
Just when I figured I'd have straight Fs
in physical fitness,
the school board decided to revoke the
rule about wearing gym suits.
Yeahhh!
Of course, I still look like a Polish sausage in my shorts,
but at least I have a choice.

Boys

BOYS,
BOYS, BOYS, BOYS,
BOYS, BOYS, BOYS, BOYS, BOYS, BOYS
that's all I think about!
I'm going to get a new hobby
just as soon as I have time
to think about something besides
BOYS.

Lunchroom

I was so hungry
I could have eaten my algebra book.
I smelled what we were having
before I even saw it.
Mystery Meat, green mushy peas,
instant potatoes with lumpy gravy,
bread pudding, and milk.
It's a good thing I like milk.

My Mirror Lies to Me

My mirror lies to me,
it whispers,
YOU ARE FAT, FAT, FAT.

I starve myself into
skeletal thinness to
the alarm of my loved ones,
crumbs fill me up like a Thanksgiving feast
and are purged from my
stomach with medicines.

I stick my finger down
my throat after a meal
of half of a half of a cracker
and yet,
my mirror still whispers FAT, FAT, FAT.

I've almost killed myself in the pursuit
of perfection,
only to find out that
what I'm really starving for
is love.

Black Barbie Doll

I'm tired of you calling me a
blackbarbiedoll
because most of my friends are white
and I get good grades
and I talk "proper,"
whatever that means.
This is me, this is how I want to be.
Nobody is going to squeeze me into
a box labeled
black or white.
Okay?

Nonconformist

I don't want to be anybody
but myself.
So, I shaved little lines
in my head and
dyed my hair purple
and green
(with just a hint of orange)
and pierced my nose and
hung a gold earring in it,
AS AN EXPRESSION OF WHO I AM
(who am I?).
Of course,
I waited until someone else did it first.
I didn't want anyone to think I'm
weird.
You know what I mean?

The Bogeyman

My mother used to tell me about the bogeyman
so I would stay in bed at night.
But since I ran away from home
and started living on the streets
I've met the *real*
BOGEYMAN.
I wish I was back home
in my own bed.

Pea Brain

At our school
it's cool to be
stupid.
I don't tell anyone
I make straight A's.
I don't know why
most guys prefer to think
that your brain is
the size of a pea.
Can I help it if
my name is permanently
engraved on the
honor roll?

In the Bathroom Mirror

In the bathroom mirror
I am transformed.
Sometimes,
I have muscles that pop out like THE HULK's.
Sometimes,
I'm a secret agent trained in karate.
My chops and kicks look great
in the bathroom mirror.
Sometimes,
I'm Kool Baby Kool,
the rock star,
master of the air guitar.
When I play
the chicks swoon and sway
and scream my name
and . . .
this daydream has been temporarily interrupted.
My little sister is screaming at me
because she has to use the bathroom.
Okay! Okay, I'm coming out.

I Was Born at the Wrong Time

I had to ask
my mom
to define
a "sit-in."
You know, they sit in a place
to protest something,
carry signs, and get arrested.
I had to ask about it
because I was born at the wrong time.
All the excitement is over with.
My mom had already marched for civil rights,
sung WE SHALL OVERCOME,
shouted BLACK POWER,
MARCHED ON WASHINGTON,
had a basketball-sized Afro,
sang sweet soul music,
and cried over
Martin Luther King Jr. and both Kennedys
long before my first birthday.
I wonder if there will be any causes left
to believe in
by the time I'm old enough
to join in the fight?

Mom Says

Mom says
"Be careful!"
"Where are you going?"
"What time are you coming home?"
I say
"I know what I'm doing!"
"Quit treating me like I'm a baby!"

I guess we keep telling each other
the same old things
in the same old way
because
we're too scared to say
I love you.

Sunglasses

I wear these dark glasses
because they're really cool
(and because I don't want you to see
the fear
in my eyes).
I walk like I do
because
I'm trying to keep
from running.
I try to stay alive with a rap
style that drives 'em wild
with what I say each and every day
because
no one seems to
understand me
when I'm talking anyway.

Forever

You told me that we were going
to be together
forever.
You said that I was yours
and you were mine
forever.
You said that you were going
to love me
forever.
I wish you would have told me that
forever
is only
three months long.

Binky

My mom cleaned my room yesterday.
I didn't notice anything important was missing
until that night.
She threw away Binky!
How could she throw Binky away!
I know he was leaking stuffing,
and one ear was missing
(I cut it off when I was pretending to be a doctor),
and his white fur had turned
a pale shade of gray,
but he's mine and I love him.
I can't sleep without him.
I crept downstairs with a flashlight
and went outside.
There was Binky, sitting on the trash heap.
I rescued him and crept back upstairs.
I slept great,
and so did Binky.
From now on, I'm hiding him in the closet.

The Tryouts

This is the most important day
of my entire life.
Cheerleader tryouts.
I've practiced until I'm
practically hoarse.
I've bounced, done the splits,
turned cartwheels, and
smiled until all my
muscles froze
in one huge cramp.
I had to bathe in liniment.
Oh no, they're calling my name.
Where are my pom-poms?
YEAAAH, TEAMMMMMM!

A Whole New Look

I got my braces taken off on Tuesday.
I got my hair cut and a curly perm on Wednesday.
I got contacts on Thursday.
Friday when I went to school
no one knew who I was.

Wait for Me

The world is full of trash,
the government is running out of cash,
people sleep on the streets
like the pavement is their
own private bedroom.
A nuclear bomb will probably kill us all
before I can get my driver's license.
But I haven't given up hope.
If I can just get out of high school
I'm going to change the world!

Career Day

Tables of smiling adults
with brochures about
engineering, medical technology,
law school, teaching, and
hundreds of jobs of all types.
Nothing
appealed to me.
Does this mean
that I'm going to make a career
out of doing nothing?

I Really Haven't Thought About It

Why is it that adults always ask you
the same question
in different ways?
"What are you going to do when you grow up?"
"Decided on a career yet?"
How can I plan a lifetime
when I haven't even decided
what I want to wear tomorrow?

Immune

I am young.
Therefore,
I am immune
to
AIDS
WAR
CANCER
AND OTHER DEADLY
ILLNESSES
and those WEIRD THINGS that happen to
other people
on TV.
I am young, and
strong, and alive.
Nothing can happen to me.
The only thing I haven't figured out is . . .
why do they make
coffins
in different sizes?

Safety

I'm really kind of afraid to graduate.
I feel safe in high school.
Who knows what will happen when all this is over?
They allow you to screw up when you're just a kid.
It's sort of expected of you.
But they don't make allowances
for adults.

The Test

I passed the written part just fine.
I practically had the whole book memorized.
I knew when to yield, when to stop, how to signal,
and all that stuff.
Then came the driver's test.
I was so nervous I could barely hold the wheel.
The officer who was riding with me
was a big guy with a big gun.
I wonder if he shoots you if you make an illegal turn?
Everything was going pretty good,
but then he asked me to parallel park.
I hate parallel parking. I can never get it right.
I gave him a sickly grin.
He didn't smile, he just rubbed the handle of his gun.
That was the best parallel parking I've ever done.
It's amazing what you can do
when you're under pressure.

Babies

I wanted a baby because
I wanted something of my very own
to love.
I never thought I'd have twins.
I didn't know how much little,
helpless babies need you.
Day and night, night and day,
it seems like I'm climbing a
mountain of disposable diapers.
All I do is sterilize bottles
and wipe butts.
I never have any fun anymore.
Who wants a double date with a couple of infants?

I'm Not Jealous

I'm not jealous of my sister.
I'm really not.
I think it's great that she's
so little and cute
(although when we stand side by side
I look like Godzilla).
Just because her hair and clothes
are always perfect
(and I always look like an unmade bed)
and she makes nothing lower than an A
(and I rejoice over Cs)
and people always say in that
disbelieving tone of voice,
"Are you really sisters?!?"
It doesn't make me jealous.
Not at all, not one little bit.
Really, it doesn't.
I AM NOT JEALOUS!

Chemical Cocoon

Every morning, I carefully wrap myself up
in a chemical cocoon.
I don't want to feel anything
I don't want to hear anything
I don't want to learn anything new.
I know enough about this old world.
It's nothing but a big ball of pain.
Maybe, one of these days
I'll emerge from all this
whole and beautiful
just like a butterfly.
If I live that long.

The Basket

I've been sitting on the bench almost the whole season.
Finally, the coach sent me in.
Some big guy practically mopped the court with me
so the referee called a foul.
He threw the ball to me so I could shoot.
My big moment. My big chance.
I was a sweaty mess.
I bounced the ball until someone yelled
"So shoot it already!"
I gripped the ball tightly
and pumped it up through the air.
The ball landed gently on the rim of the basket,
and slid through the net. YES!
I felt great!!
I know, I know it was the last ten seconds of
the final quarter,
and we were leading 110 to 66 anyway.
But it was the most important shot of the game
to me.

Say That Again?

Like, you broke up with me
because you said that
your parents said that
we are too young
to be so serious about each other.
Since you love, love, love, love me, and will never,
ever forget me
why are you dating her?

I'm Going to Be Homecoming Queen
Even If It Kills Me

I've spent the last two weeks
being nice to everybody,
even that gross guy
in my third period class.
This is my last chance to be
HOMECOMING QUEEN.
Every vote counts.
It's so hard to be nice
when you're really not.

Colors of the Race

So, you finally found out what I knew all along.
My big full lips are beautiful
and so envied that
you pay
to have yours plumped up.
Roller coaster curves
and caramel cream to deep ebony skin tones
show off clothes to perfection.
Let's not even talk about
all the ways I can style my hair,
previously labeled as
"nappy."
Yeah, sometimes I might be loud
and unafraid to speak up for myself,
but I was raised to be proud,
no need to whisper,
or smile falsely.
I'm glad you finally realize
that all the colors of the race
are beautiful.

A Lucas • Evans Book

Text copyright © 1995 by Angela Shelf Medearis
Illustrations copyright © 1995 by Michael Bryant

Macmillan Books for Young Readers
An imprint of Simon & Schuster Children's Publishing Division
Simon & Schuster Macmillan
1230 Avenue of the Americas
New York, New York 10020

The text of this book is set in 12 pt. ITC Bookman Light.
The illustrations were done in pencil.

Printed and bound in the United States of America.

First edition

1 3 5 7 9 10 8 6 4 2

LIBRARY OF CONGRESS CATALOGING-IN-PUBLICATION DATA
Medearis, Angela Shelf
Skin deep and other teenage reflections : poems / by Angela Shelf Medearis ;
illustrated by Michael Bryant.   p.   cm.
Summary: An insightful collection of easy-to-read poems about the problems and
frustrations of being a teenager.
ISBN 0-02-765980-1
1. Teenagers—Poetry.   2. Young adult poetry, American.
[1. Adolescence—Poetry.   2. American poetry.]   I. Bryant, Michael, ill.   II. Title.
PS3563.E2384S58   1995   811'.54—dc20   94-19928

poems by Angela Shelf Medearis

Skin deep

and Other Teenage Reflections

illustrated by Michael Bryant

Macmillan Books for Young Readers • New York